THE **BIG** BOOK OF Early Phonics

Prim-Ed Publishing

by Betty Pollard

The Big Book of Early Phonics

FOREWORD

The activities in this book are consistent and can be used to introduce and consolidate three-letter blends and basic sounds.

The activities may be used for a whole class, in groups or as individual activities.

They allow for worksheets, blackboard and overhead projector activities.

CONTENTS

Page	Blend	Page	Blend
1	at as in cat	29	en
2	at	30	eg as in beg
3	at	31	eg
4	at	32	ed as in bed
5	am as in jam	33	ell as in bell
6	am	34	ell
7	ab as in crab	35	ot as in hot
8	ab	36	ot
9	ad as in dad	37	od as in rod
10	ag as in bag	38	op as in top
11	an as in can	39	op
12	an	40	og as in dog
13	ap as in cap	41	og
14	ap	42	ob as in cob
15	ip as in dip	43	oll as in doll
16	in as in bin	44	oll
17	in	45	ub as in tub
18	im as in dim	46	ud as in bud
19	ib as in bib	47	ug as in tug
20	ib	48	ug
21	ig as in pig	49	up as in cup
22	ig	50	um as in hum
23	id as in lid	51	un as in sun
24	ill as in hill	52	un
25	ill	53	ut as in hut
26	et as in net	54	ut
27	et	55	ull as in gull
28	en as in hen	56	x as in box

Prim-Ed Publishing

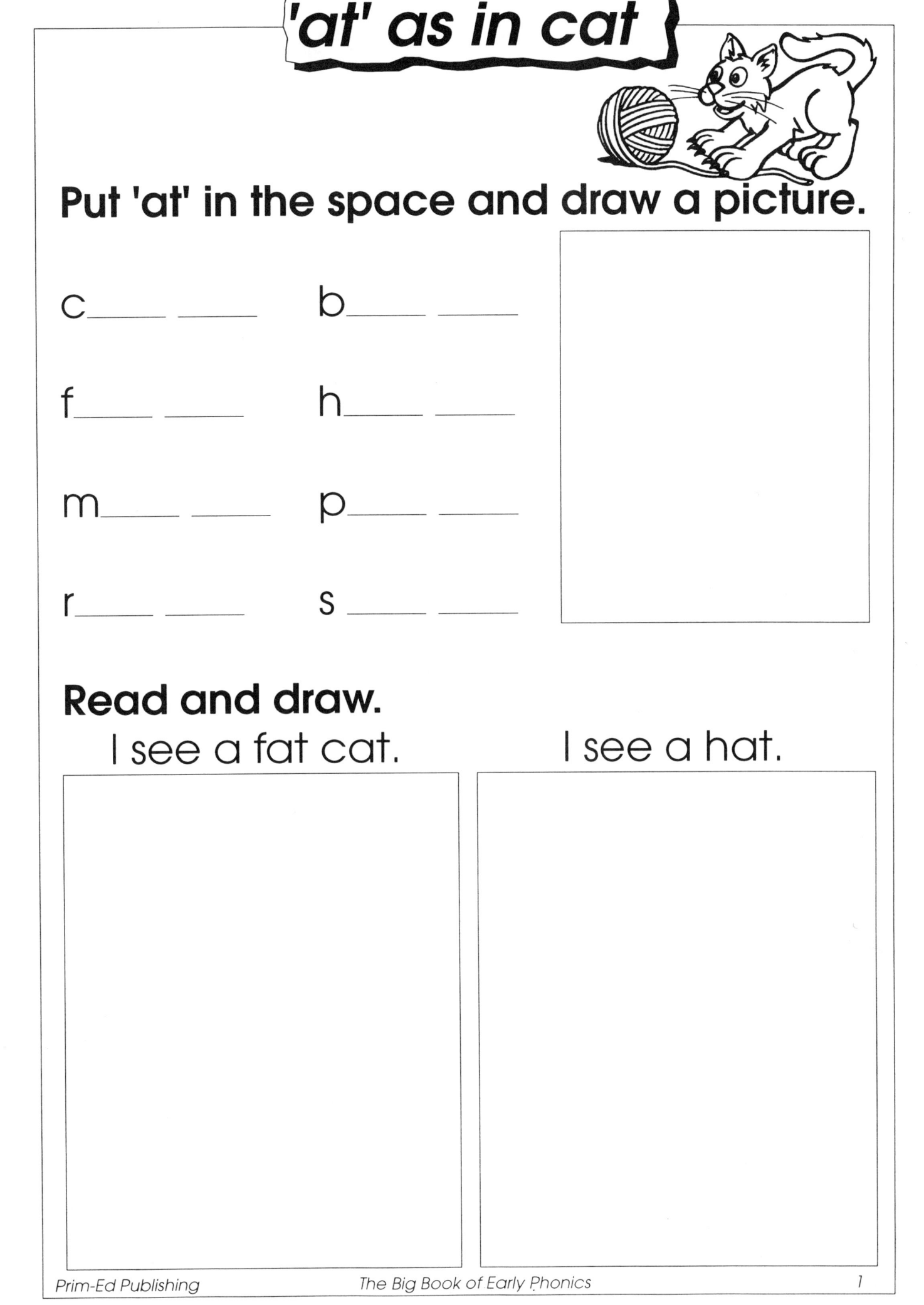

'at' as in cat

Put 'at' in the space and draw a picture.

c___ ___   b___ ___

f___ ___   h___ ___

m___ ___   p___ ___

r___ ___   s ___ ___

Read and draw.

I see a fat cat.   I see a hat.

Prim-Ed Publishing   The Big Book of Early Phonics

'at' as in cat

**Put a line under the 'at' sound.
Draw a picture of a bat.**

cat   fat

bat   hat

mat   pat

rat   sat

Yes/No

1. A cat can run. _____

2. A rat can run. _____

3. A hat can run. _____

4. A bat can run. _____

5. A mat can run. _____

'at' as in cat

Read the stories.

My cat is fat.

My cat is black.

My cat is on the mat.

My cat has a hat.

I like my cat.

Draw the cat.

'at' as in cat

Put 'at' words on the cat.
His name is Nat.
He is a fat cat.

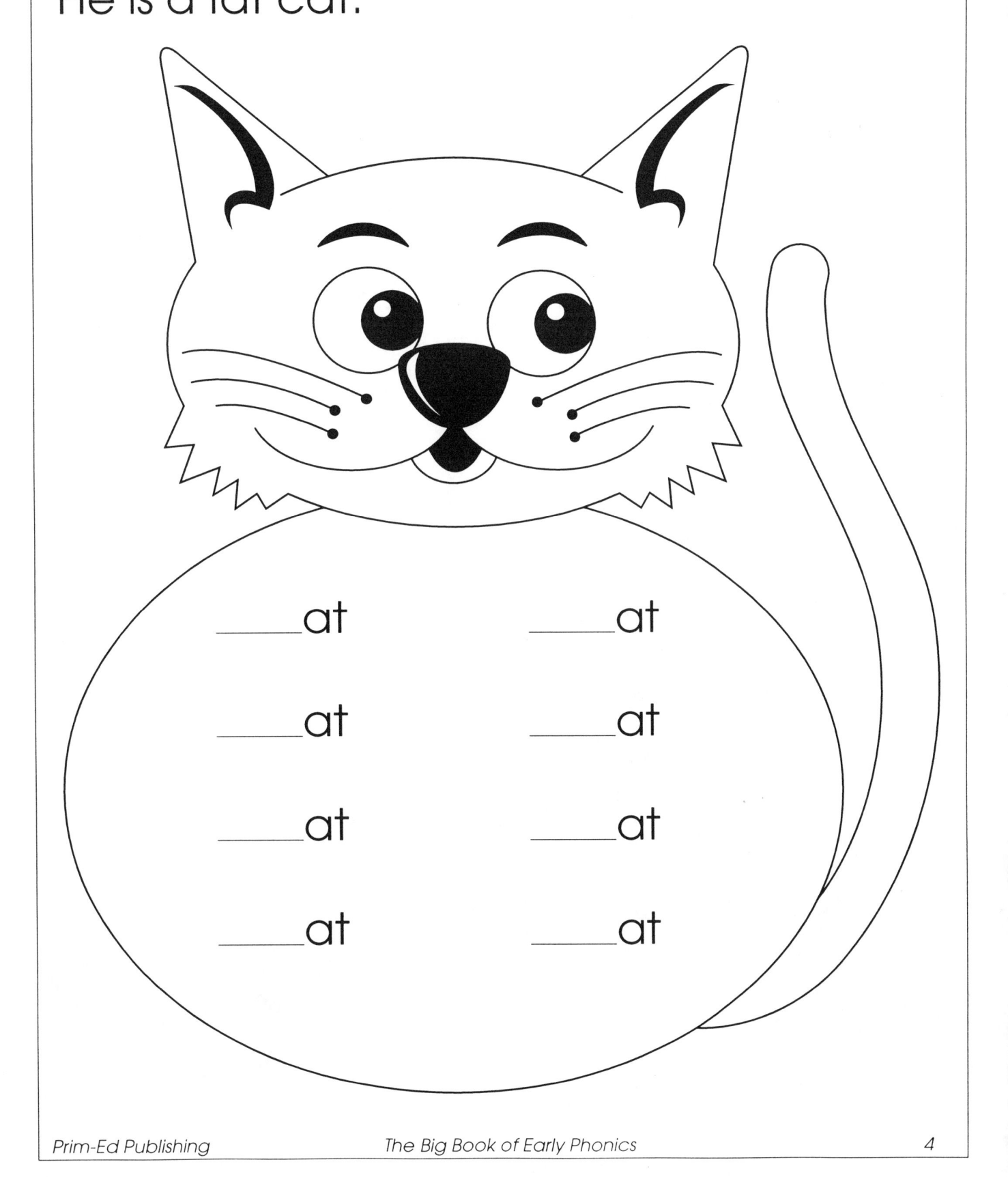

___at   ___at

___at   ___at

___at   ___at

___at   ___at

'am' as in jam

Put 'am' in the space.
Draw a picture.

h _____   j _____

P _____   r _____

S _____   d _____

Yes/No

1. Do you like jam? _____

2. Do you like ham? _____

Read and draw.

Sam and Pam sat by the dam.

'am' as in jam

Put 'am' in the space.

Strawberry Jam

d_____ ___

h_____ ___

P_____ ___

S_____ ___

r_____ ___

1. I like bread and _____ ___ ___.

2. _____ ___ ___ is a boy.

3. _____ ___ ___ is a girl.

4. A father sheep is a _____ ___ ___.

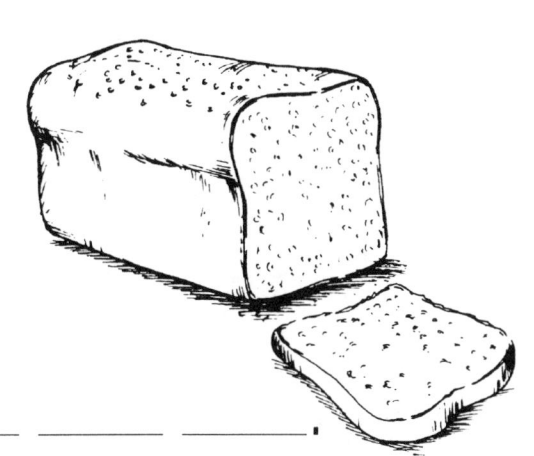

'ab' as in crab

Put 'ab' in the space.
Draw pictures for two of the words.

d____ ____   j____ ____

l____ ____   t____ ____

cr____ ____

Add 's'

crab____   tab____

Read and draw.

A man can see the crab.

The crab ran and ran.

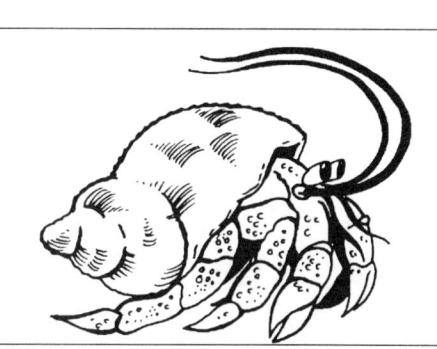

Prim-Ed Publishing   The Big Book of EARLY Phonics   7

'ab' as in cab

Put in the missing word.

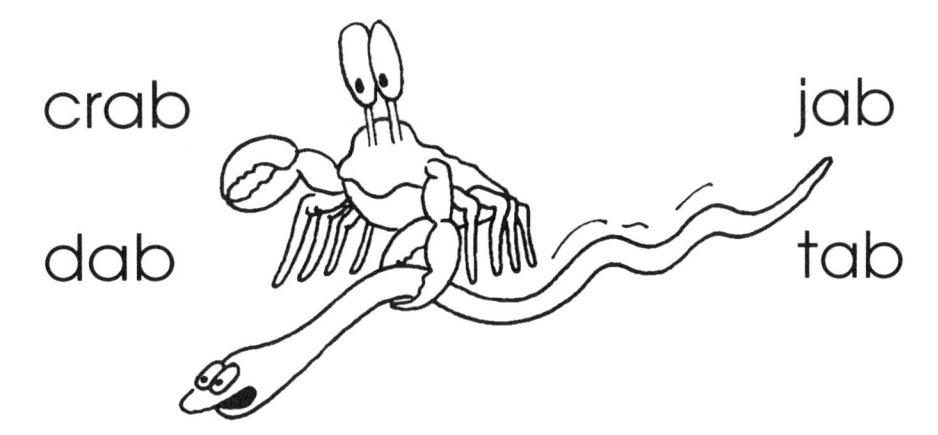

crab　　　　　　　　　　　jab

dab　　　　　　　　　　　tab

1. I caught a _____.

2. I had a _____.

Draw a crab.

'ad' as in dad

Put 'ad' in the space.

d____ ____

f____ ____

l____ ____

p____ ____

b____ ____

h____ ____

m____ ____

s____ ____

Put in the missing word.

sad	mad	pad
bad	dad	had

1. He is _____.

2. She is _____.

3. My dad _____ a van.

'ag' as in bag

Put 'ag' in the space.

b____ ____   l____ ____

r____ ____   s____ ____

t____ ____   w____ ____

Read and draw.

Mum has a bag.

My dog can wag its tail.

'an' as in can

Put 'an' in the space.

c_____ _____

D_____ _____

N_____ _____

r_____ _____

m_____ _____

f_____ _____

p_____ _____

v_____ _____

Read and draw.

A man in a van.

Dan has a can.

'an' as in can

Yes/No

1. Mum has a pan. _____

2. Do you have a pan? _____

3. Do you have a fan? _____

Put in the missing word.

| ran | fan | man |
| pan | nan | can |

The man _____ to the van.

Draw a van. Colour it blue.

'ap' as in cap

Put 'ap' in the space.

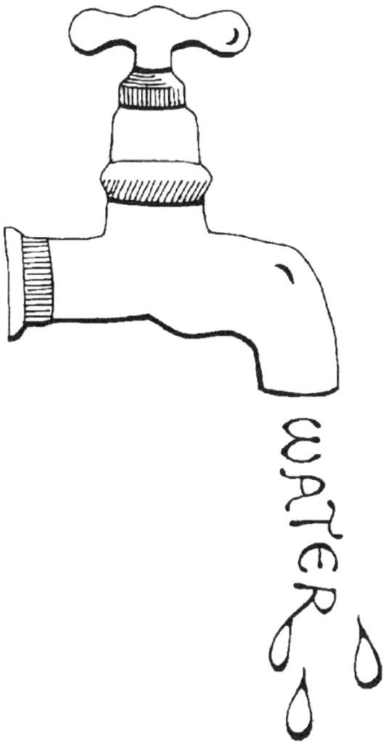

c_____   g_____

l_____   m_____

n_____   r_____

s_____   t_____

z_____

Put in the missing words.

cap   tap   lap
gap   map   nap

1. Dad has a _____.

2. Baby will have a _____.

3. Turn on the _____.

'ap' as in cap

Put the 'ap' words on the cap.

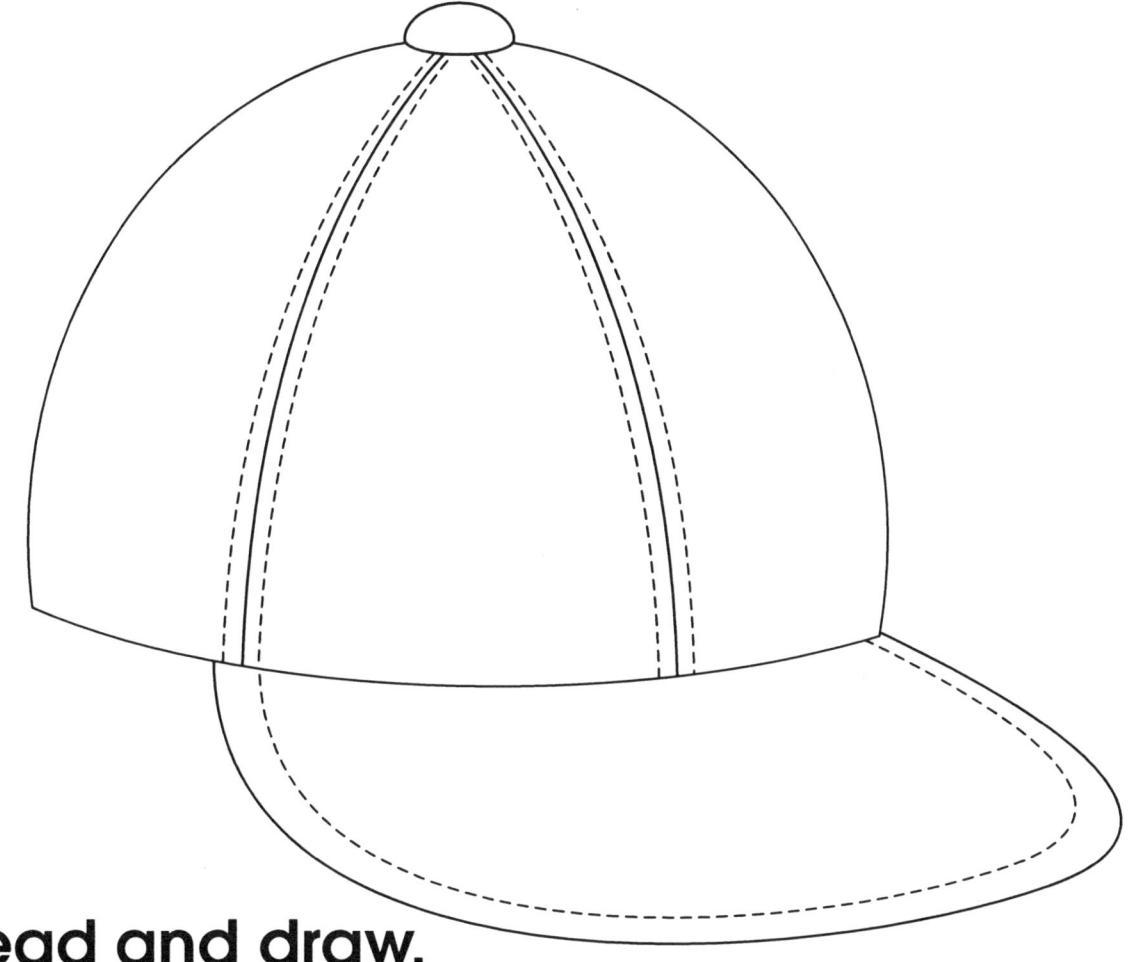

Read and draw.

A cat can lap.

The man in the van has a map.

'ip' as in dip

Put 'ip' in the space.

d____ ____   h____ ____

l____ ____   n____ ____

p____ ____   r____ ____

t____ ____   z____ ____

Yes/No

1. Can a truck tip? _____

2. Can you see a zip? _____

3. A truck has a zip. _____

4. Do you have a hip? _____

5. Can paper rip? _____

6. Do you have a lip? _____

'in' as in bin

Put 'in' in the space.

b_____ _____   f_____ _____

p_____ _____   d_____ _____

t_____ _____   w_____ _____

Yes/No

1. Can you see a bin? _____

2. Can you see a pin? _____

3. Do you make a din? _____

4. A fish has a fin. _____

5. Do you like to win? _____

6. Can food come in a tin? _____

'in' as in bin

Read and draw.

A big tin and a little tin.

A cat is by the big tin.

A rat is by the little tin.

The rat is looking at the cat.

'im' as in dim

Put 'im' in the space.

d____ ____   h____ ____

r____ ____   T____ ____

sw____ ____

Read and draw.

Tim can swim at the beach.

'ib' as in bib

Put 'ib' in the space.

b___ ___

f___ ___

n___ ___

r___ ___

Read and draw.

Draw a bib.

Put the words on the bib.

'ib' as in bib

Put in the missing word.

bib   nib   rib   ribs

1. Baby has a _____.

2. We have _____.

Yes/No

1. Do you have a bib? _____

2. Baby has a bib. _____

3. Do you have a rib? _____

Read and draw.

A baby with a bib.

'ig' as in pig

Put 'ig' in the space.

b_____ _____

d_____ _____

f_____ _____

j_____ _____

p_____ _____

w_____ _____

Put the 'ig' words in the pig.

'ig' as in pig

Yes/No

1. Do you like pigs? _____

2. Can you do a jig? _____

3. A pig has a wig. _____

4. Can a pig jig? _____

Read and draw.

A big pig and six little pigs.

A pig with
a wig.

'id' as in lid

Put 'id' in the space.

d___ ___   h___ ___

k___ ___   l___ ___

r___ ___

Read and draw.

Little Billy Goat Gruff is a kid.

The kid hid behind the bin.

'ill' as in hill

Put 'ill' in the space.

h_____ _____ _____   b_____ _____ _____

f_____ _____   k_____ _____ _____

m_____ _____ _____   p_____ _____ _____

s_____ _____ _____   t_____ _____ _____

w_____ _____ _____

Put the words on the hill.
Draw Jack and Jill going up the hill.

'ill' as in hill

Put in the missing word.

Jill	hill	mill
bill	fill	kill
pill	sill	till

1. Jack and _____ went up the hill.

2. A duck has a _____.

3. The Little Red Hen went to the _____.

Draw a windmill.

'et' as in net

**Put 'et' in the space.
Draw a picture.**

n___ ___   j___ ___

b___ ___   g___ ___

l___ ___   m___ ___

s___ ___   p___ ___

Read and draw.

A wet day.

A pet in a jet.

'et' as in net

Put 'et' words in the raindrops.

'en' as in hen

Put 'en' in the space. Draw pictures for two of the words.

h___ ___   d___ ___

B___ ___   p___ ___

t___ ___   m___ ___

h___ ___ ___s

Read and draw.

Ten men by a jet.

'en' as in hen

Read and draw.

A big fat hen.
The hen has ten eggs.

Yes/No

1. Ben is a girl's name. _____

2. A fox has a den. _____

3. We have ten legs. _____

4. We write with a pen. _____

5. A hen lays eggs. _____

'eg' as in beg

Put 'eg' in the space.

b_____ _____   k_____ _____

l_____ _____   p_____ _____

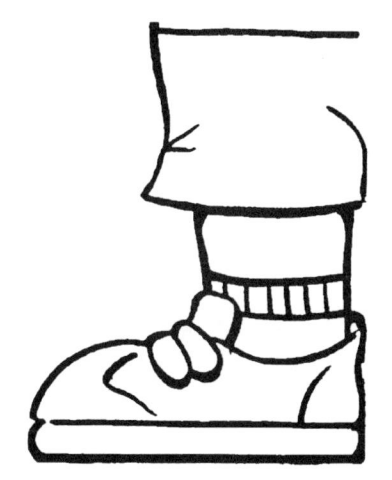

Add 's' to the words.

beg_____   leg_____

peg_____   keg_____

Draw ten pegs.

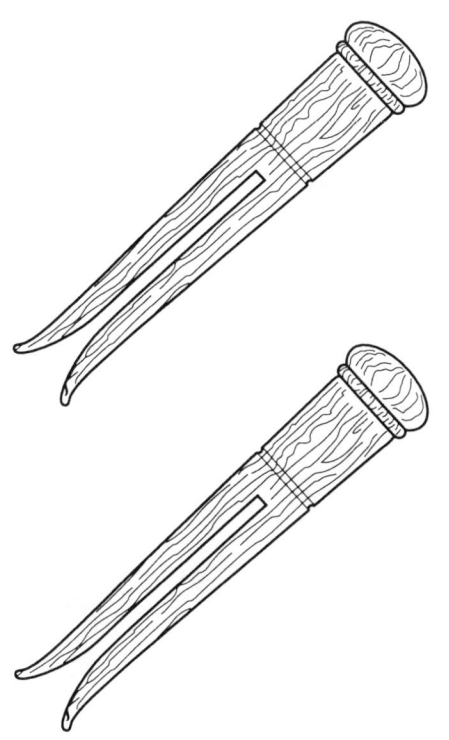

'eg' as in beg

Put in the missing word.

leg   peg   beg   keg

legs   pegs   kegs

1. A dog can _____.

2. A dog has four _____.

3. I have two _____.

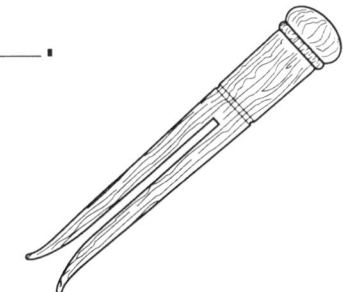

Read and draw.

A dog can beg.

A peg is by the dog.

'ed' as in bed

Put 'ed' in the space.

b_____   f_____

l_____   r_____

T_____   w_____

Read and draw.

Draw a bed.
Put big Ted in the bed.
Colour the bed red.

'ell' as in bell

Put 'ell' in the space.

Draw a picture for two of the words.

b___ ___ ___   f___ ___ ___

s___ ___ ___   d___ ___ ___

t___ ___ ___   w___ ___ ___

y___ ___ ___   sm___ ___ ___

Read and draw.

A bell on the well.

'ell' as in bell

Put in the missing word.

bell   sell   smell

yell   fell   dell

tell   well

1. Jack and Jill went to the _____.

2. Do not _____.

3. We can _____ flowers.

4. Jack _____ down.

5. We will _____ a story.

6. We can ring the _____.

7. Can I _____ my old toys?

'ot' as in hot

Put 'ot' in the space.
Draw pictures for three of the words.

h___ ___   c___ ___

d___ ___   g___ ___

j___ ___   l___ ___

n___ ___   p___ ___

r___ ___

Yes/No

1. Can a pot hop? _____

2. Is it hot today? _____

3. The sun is hot today. _____

4. Can you make a dot? _____

5. Do you sleep in a cot? _____

'ot' as in hot

Put the 'ot' words on the pot.

Read and draw.

Draw a baby in a cot.   Draw a hot pot.

'od' as in rod

Put 'od' in the space.
Draw two of the pictures.

c____ ____   n____ ____

p____ ____   r____ ____

Yes/No

1. A cod is a fish. _____

2. We catch fish with a rod. _____

3. Can you nod your head? _____

4. Peas are in a pod. _____

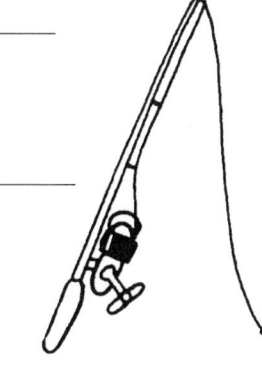

Read and draw.

A fishing rod with a cod fish.

'op' as in top

Put 'op' in the space.
Draw a picture.

h_____ ___

m_____ ___

t_____ ___

st_____ ___

Put in the missing word.

hop   top   mop   pop   stop

1. A car can _____.

2. The cleaner has a _____.

3. A _____ can spin.

4. Popcorn goes _____.

'op' as in top

Yes/No

1. Can you hop? _____

2. Popcorn goes pop. _____

3. Can you mop the floor? _____

5. Can a car stop? _____

Read and draw.
A coloured spinning top.

'og' as in dog

Put 'og' in the space.
Draw pictures of some of the words.

d___ ___   b___ ___

f___ ___   h___ ___

j___ ___   c___ ___

l___ ___   fr___ ___

Read and draw.

A frog on a log.   A dog is by the log.

'og' as in dog

Put in the missing word.

jog   bog   dog   log

cog   fog   hog   frog

1. A _____ can jump.

2. It is fun to _____.

3. My pet is a _____.

4. A _____ is like a pig.

Yes/No

1. Can you jog? _____

2. Do you like hogs? _____

3. A frog can hop. _____

4. A dog can jog. _____

Prim-Ed Publishing   The Big Book of Early Phonics   41

'ob' as in cob

Put 'ob' in the space.

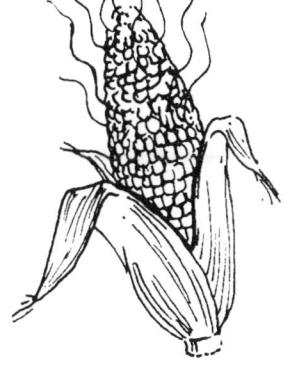

B_____ _____

c_____ _____

j_____ _____

m_____ _____

s_____ _____

h_____ _____

b_____ _____

Add 's' to the words.

sob____   cob____   job____

Read and draw.

A cob of corn.

'oll' as in doll

Put 'oll' in the space.

d_____ _____ _____

r_____ _____ _____

tr_____ _____ _____

Read and draw.

A troll under the bridge.

A doll on a bed.

'oll' as in doll

Yes/No

1. Can you eat a roll? _____

2. Can you roll down a hill? _____

3. Can a doll roll? _____

4. Can a troll roll? _____

Add 's'

doll_____   roll_____   troll_____

Read and draw.

Six little trolls on a hill.

'ub' as in tub

Put 'ub' in the space.

Draw pictures for two of the words..

c___ ___

h___ ___

r___ ___

s___ ___

t___ ___

Read and draw.

A cub in a tub.

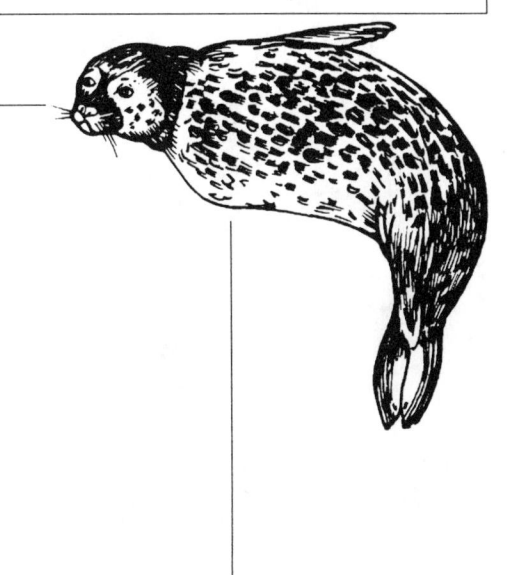

'ud' as in bud

Put 'ud' in the space.
Draw some of the pictures.

b___ ___

c___ ___

b___ ___ s

d___ ___

s___ ___ s

m___ ___

Read and draw.

Suds in a tub.

Ten pretty buds.

'ug' as in tug

Put 'ug' in the space.
Draw some of the pictures.

t___ ___

b___ ___

h ___ ___

j___ ___

m___ ___

r___ ___

Yes/No

1. A tug is a strong boat. _____

2. We drink from a mug. _____

'ug' as in tug

Read and draw.

A tugboat by a ship.

A blue jug.

A red and yellow bug.

'up' as in cup

Put 'up' in the space.
Draw pictures.

c_____

p_____

c_____ ___s

p_____ ___s

Read and draw.

Seven cups. Colour five blue and two yellow.

Ten pups in a box.

'um' as in hum

Put 'um' in the space.
Draw a picture.

h___ ___

g___ ___

s___ ___

m___ ___

dr___ ___

Yes/No

1. I like sums. _____

2. A drum is fun. _____

3. Can you hum? _____

4. I help my mum. _____

5. Can you do this sum? 1+1= ☐ _____

'un' as in sun

Put 'un' in the space.
Draw some pictures.

s_____

b_____

f_____

g_____

n_____

r_____

Read and draw.

It is fun to run.					The sun is hot.

'un' as in sun

Put the 'un' words on the sun.

Yes/No

The sun is hot. _____

You eat a bun. _____

Can you run? _____

'ut' as in hut

Put 'ut' in the space.
Draw three of the pictures.

h___ ___

c___ ___   b___ ___

n ___ ___   r___ ___

Yes/No

1. Do you like nuts? _____

2. Scissors can cut. _____

3. Do you live in a hut? _____

Add 's' to the words.

nut____   hut____   cut____

'ut' as in hut

Read and draw.

Nine nuts in a bag.

A hut by a tree.

I can cut.

'ull' as in gull

Put 'ull' in the space.
Draw pictures.

d___ __ __

h___ __ __

g___ __ __

Yes/No

1. The sky is dull. _____

2. A gull is a bird. _____

3. A boat has a hull. _____

Read and draw.
Seagulls are flying in the sky.

'x' as in box

Put 'x' in the space.
Draw two of the pictures.

wa____   Ma____

si____   fi____

mi____   bo____

fo____

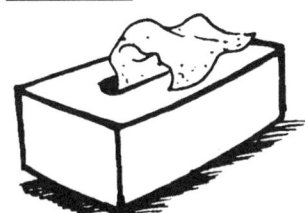

Read and draw.

A fox on a box.

Max is six.